Introduction

What is that furry animal climbing in the night?
Perhaps it is raccoon. Let's explore the
wonderful world of raccoons.

What Animal Class Do Raccoons Belong To?

Raccoons belong to the animal class of mammals. Mammals are warm-blooded animals that have hair or fur, give birth to live young, and females produce milk to feed their young.

Amazing Pictures and Facts About Raccoons

By: Mina Kelly

What Do Raccoons Eat?

Raccoons are omnivores. Omnivores are animals that eat plants and meat. Raccoons love to eat fish, but when they are unable to find meat they will scavenge and eat whatever they can find. Even from your garbage can!

Do Raccoons Forage For Food?

Raccoons forage (or search) for their food and are often found living near water. Raccoons have even been observed washing their food before they eat it!

How Many Species of Raccoons Exist?

There are ten different species of raccoons living in the world. Although they vary in size, their appearance is the same amongst different species.

Where Do Raccoons Live?

Raccoons are native to North America. However, they have been deliberately introduced to other countries and can be found in Europe and Japan.

What Do Raccoons Look Like?

Raccoons are medium-sized, grey animals with a thick layer of fur covering their body. They have long black and grey striped tails and are recognized for the distinctive black mask that surrounds their eyes.

Do Raccoons Have Hands?

Raccoons have four feet, with five toes on both their front and hind feet. Their front feet are very similar to human hands in both appearance and dexterity.

How Big Are Raccoons?

Raccoons are medium-sized mammals that grown between 16-28 inches, weighing between 7-19 pounds. Male raccoons are larger than females.

What Habitat Do Raccoons Require?

Raccoons naturally inhabit wooded areas. However, they are very adaptable and can live in mountainous regions and wetter habitats. As their habitats are destroyed for human development, they have been known to the live in the resulting urban areas.

Are Raccoons Fast?

Raccoons can reach top speeds of 15 miles per hour. That is faster than a human can run!

Can Raccoons Climb?

Raccoons are excellent climbers. They are often found climbing or hiding high above in the treetops.

Are Raccoons Social Animals?

Raccoons are solitary animals. The only social groups they form consist of a female raccoon and her young.

Are Raccoons Nocturnal Animals?

Raccoons are nocturnal animals. Nocturnal animals are most active during the night. However, it is not uncommon to see a raccoon during the day.

Do Raccoons Have Natural Enemies?

Bobcats, foxes, wolves and mountain lions prey on raccoons. Raccoons will attack their enemies when they feel threatened.

What Is the Lifespan of A Raccoon?

Raccoons live between 5-16 years in the wild. They can survive much longer in captivity, up to 25 years.

What Are Baby Raccoons Called?

Baby raccoons are called 'kits.' Kits are born blind and deaf. All raccoons are born with their distinctive black eye mask.

How Many Teeth Do Raccoons Have?

Raccoons have 40 teeth, including four long and sharp canine teeth at the front of their mouth. They use their teeth to chew their food before they swallow it.

What Is the Raccoons Relationship To Humans?

Many people keep raccoons as pets. This is inadvisable, as raccoons are wild animals. Raccoons have been known to carry rabies. If a human comes in contact with a raccoon and is scratched or bitten, they should seek medical attention.

Do Raccoons Have Night Vision?

Raccoons have excellent night vision. Often, when you see their eyes at night, they appear reflective.

Conservation Status

Despite habitat destruction, raccoon population numbers are on the rise. They are listed as "least concern" in terms of potential endangered status.

42244765R00015